For QP

Published by Auntie Press

Acknowledgements

Early versions of "Our white blinds," "Two a.m.," "Reading Nella Larsen," "All the serious problems I have summed up in one poem," and "Q & P" appeared in *The New Engagement*. "Blue invincibility" appeared in *The Gay & Lesbian Review*. I am grateful to all the friends and acquaintances whose generosity, voices, and bottom natures found their way into this book. Special thanks to Iris Cushing for editorial expertise. To Patrick James who encouraged me to share these poems with the world. To Michael Hofmann for his tender designs. To Todd Shalom for his sympathetic ear. To Ivy Baldwin & co. for movement. To Jeremy Laverdure for the gift of Jill Johnston. To Jennifer Alberghini and the students at Queens College for discerning feedback. To Gertrude Stein for paying no mind to the haters. And to Mark for demonstrating fearlessness, time after time after time.

There is a complicated history of them to me then when there is of them a completed understanding of the bottom nature of them ...

Gertrude Stein

Blue invincibility

Standing in line at the pharmacy
  singing "Glor-ee-uh,"
daily dose of the real   trendy
  pills.

Harm reduction dreams of no harm
no foul   I take these
  for both of us.

Up at the house it's called a *soupe de noeuds*!
Have faith   everybody
  wins.

A purple annulated case in white ladybugs
  and braille,
seven slots   for seven
  lovers.

We have been prematurely old
  for a long time now,
but you really won't remember
what it was like   to be
  a boy

      insomnia

till sunrise because you thought
  you had AIDS
listening to Amy Grant   praying
  to be saved.

But sexual panics pass,
forced blooms   take
  care.

The pharmakon is calling

(second wind
 second act
 second coming)

calling Gloria.

Run the dishwasher at night

so that it hums

run the dishwasher at night
so that it runs
& so

the dishwasher runs at night

So it hums

I love this dishwasher
I fight for this dishwasher
I struggle for it
I fill it and I empty it
I buy it soap
I run it at night

Swish and soap and swish
& swish and swishy soap
& swish and suds and sudsy soap
& soap and soapy suds
& swishy swirl oh gurl and whirl
& whirly girly whirly whirl
& whirl and soap and swish and soap
& swish and soap and soap and soap
& suds and suds and so and suds
& so and soap and soap and suds
& so asleep and soap asleep
& so and soap and soap and pause

I need these dishes
& these washes
& this water

It is a question of comfort and being
& being lulled

I buy it soap
& run it at night

    it hums
whirs
runs
comforts
cleans

it comforts and cleans
& lulls

It puts the world together while we sleep

Rototiller
For Ivy Baldwin

Plowed earth
the old twentieth century way.
Spring garden. You grip your steed
in old jeans and muddy sneakers.
When the blades strike root
  or rock
        the beast leaps forward,
       jerking you behind it,
     fire hydrant red
       bucking bronco.
  You don't let go.

This is not a drive-in movie theater or rodeo;
there are no trailers, no bales of sweet and sour hay
piled up against the concession stand, no
soft drinks sweating in wax paper cups, no
baby blue perforated tickets torn apart
for raffles or general admissions, no creep
creeping out behind the port-a-potty, no
  clowns, no
        bulls, no
       parked cars to park in, no
     explicit teenage couples
       necking in the complicit shadow
  of the upper row.

There is only you, the rotating teeth
of the rented braying machine
chewing up the front lawn,
your parents looking on,
and me, watching you just happen
  to be
        the ambient cowboy
     we never
    stopped
     rooting
      for.

Some home goods

If you counted the pillows

in this room
the cartilage of a dog's ear
and two African masks

A tape dispenser

clear shell
two ears glued
together empty

Red rubber boots

on a bear
in the living room
the night John moved in

Queen pillow

Home Goods
a wrinkle peals across
   the Q
          in burlap

DANGER MEN WORKING

that sign
had a hot water bath
four walls ago

A scarf

Mayan skirt
green-gold blue snake
around my neck

Writing implements

musical arrangements
domestic puzzles
of things

Composition as

middle-class aesthetics
this Muji pen is through a cloud
of vapor

Kitchens are

where grievances murmur
between glances at a recipe
for peach and blackberry pie.

You tell me "Not one pie,
two"; that filo dough
is not pie crust.

Friendship—these two plums are rotten
("don't say 'rancid'") —measured in crumbs
and last night's lines of coke.

A little dog is

                    a stitched-up sack after surgery.

Two thousand dollars,
two chunks of undigested carrot
quarantined in the upper intestines.

What's a little debt
compared to the cost of not being solicitous
to a needy creature?

We complain,
but we care and persevere, and in the end
we'll have done the right thing.

The little sock seems appreciative,
eats her meals, now, and keeps the carrots down.

Tonight we'll lay untroubled heads,
trusting our feet to the rolled-up warmth
of a darned dog.

Routine

Working out arguments in the shower in the morning,
the mind's machinery drums through wet noise,
phrase after phrase.

> Not clarity, but cog work—the
> soul clicks, sagacious; analysis and
> cleanliness, standing body, moving
> soap, running water.

A splash hits my naked
shoulder   and bursts
into sunstones lit by
the narrow window.

> They fall away with the
> waterfall, swallowed by
> the spiral that slakes the
> drain and sucks the world
> with it.

Teabag

flirting with the rim
of a plate; prune skin
or chewed tobacco
dressed in a tinted
wet silk shirt.

Used, cold, smug clump
of shredded leaf;
ready or not — another dip
in the mug's finely
incurved lips.

Concentric spill;
watercolor rings
around the saucer,
like the bottom half
of a lower-case *a*
blown out
in cream china.

Two a.m.

He has a swallowtail butterfly in his mouth
He knows I'm here,
   he undresses,
      he talks

Truth, somewhere between the cloaca
   and the cochlea

My head dampens pillows

I don't want to kill him,
   and yet he lives —
      you live

Soberly I drove us home
   from the wedding party
      where you gave the bartender your number
        and I stood next to the fire escape ladder
          watching modern dancers dance
                        in circular ceremony,
                          gathering distances
                             with disciplined limbs

   They served a cocoa cake,
      raspberry liqueur,
        wet sponge

At two a.m.
   after a wedding party
      you have a black-yellow butterfly on your tongue

   Sleep infects what remains
      of sense

      and I have the car keys
        and your tongue and my ear
         in our bedroom

Dermatitis

If we died
and they broke into our apartment and entered our bedroom
they would find seven different kinds of lotion

and they would think of our skin
and how dry we were

Childcare

You cry at every opportunity
My name — digestible vessel of your distress

A doula has tied steak knives to your elbows and knees with cord
and the severed heads of forks have been stabbed into your ankles
so that you have spurs

I want to console you
and hold you until the monsters retreat
I don't know if I can afford another night
of this blood drive

Bedbug

From behind —
you've found a new way
     to bite,
drunk honesty.

It was two a.m. again.
You crawled into bed
     and drew blood,
and all my fears
     rushed out.

You in the morning;
a monument to rest —
no stain,
     nothing to bleach.

Bedsprung

Apple blossoms dropped
in the shape of a hoop skirt —
dirt pink delicates.

One day of rain

is appreciated

when it coincides
with the end of a conference
or when

you've had conference
with a banana in a can

bruised

soft skin browned
at the bottom

Long distance

You must be smoking under wisteria plumes
blowing fragrant cradles over the arbor edge

You keep the secret of the Northeast in your cigarette
and those impostor pictures of the dead

Vacancy calls collect, your voice a summer resort,
like the one from *Dirty Dancing*

Fidelity between bells of wisteria and the drone
of an angry air conditioner in Queens

Substitute children—we will never witness
the graduation of the trees we planted

You have a recipe in your hand
for talking out the jealousies—ice clinks and cherries,
Manhattan, sweet bitters

Our white blinds

are always in some position
are always shut or almost shut
are always open
  in some position

Our blinds are always opening
  and shutting in position

in white
in closing
positioning the light
  above the bed

Reading Nella Larsen

I saw you in the restaurant, in the
library, in the hospital, sitting back
with your typewriter, knowing all the
bullshit that people serve, and writing
down your infamy—a burden worth
walking away from when it stopped
being fun—when the flirtation with
notoriety drew more than narcissi on
a summer dress in Chicago—when
people had forgotten how to read and
everything just fell—

Sargasso

To be white people dancing
in the middle of the floor
at an after-party for black queers
is a faux pas
in which apology entangles with plea—

the way plastic refuse
assembles in desert island swirls
that currents have carved
for centuries
at the center of a sea

Precedent set

Madison Keys smiles like
every girl I ever went to
high school with

Not every girl
just the rich girls
who lived in big houses
and drove white VW convertible
Rabbits

and had kind and intelligent
dads with arm hair who made
lots of money and moms who
made sure everything was right
and volunteered at school

I probably had a crush
on you and was jealous
of you at the same time

I know who your boyfriend was

I can see all the love all
the security and support
and self-esteem in those
buck teeth those beautiful
teeth those white teeth those
untainted teeth

Three white men talking about identity politics at a bookstore in Saugerties, NY

I'm browsing Psychology. High school kids play chess nearby. Three white men sit in a triangle of lounge chairs in the center of the bookstore.

One of them is concerned. One of them is a Film Studies professor. One of them understands a trans student's complaint, but disagrees with the firing of the professor.

Their voices are library-low, the talk deliberate. There is sympathy and frustration and tension. They are at no point not taking this seriously. They have read Zadie Smith.

One of them wonders:
What's a trigger warning?

This scene has never felt more fragile — or necessary — as though one had wandered into a nursery and found a child spellbound by a puzzle, absorbed by the horizon of solving it. One word could break the whole thing.

A diligent clerk passes them, returning books to Women's Studies. The disinterested high school kids are laughing. I'm monitoring the situation from Philosophy.

Sitting at my desk waiting for better things to happen

All the serious problems I have summed up in one poem

I had decided to stay out of the latest Facebook debate, but in the end I couldn't help myself. It seemed urgent and I was drinking cold coffee and ordering Seamless. I put a lot of energy into that post just to make sure that I'd done the work and to minimize the chance of being misread or attacked or called out for being racist or misogynistic or neoliberal or heteronormative or homonormative. I typed it on the screen and deleted it and retyped it and reworded it and deleted specific words and put them back and deleted them again. I thought about the world. I thought about other people. I thought about other points of view in relation to my own point of view and I typed it into the screen and made some final changes and reread it many times and it looked good to me and so I posted it. The buzzer rang and my delivery came. Not having to exchange money directly with the delivery person makes it feel like they've showed up with free food, so I felt momentarily guilty about not giving her a cash tip even though I knew I'd already given her twenty per cent through the app. She handed me the heavy bag and we both smiled and bowed and nodded and she went on her way and I locked the door behind her. I sat down on the sofa and pulled out my food, setting the plastic and paper containers onto the glass counterpane of the coffee table. I turned on the television and started an episode of *Buffy the Vampire Slayer* and paused it, because before I'd eaten a single piece of Pad See Ew I checked my phone to see if there had been any response to my post. My stomach sank when I saw the little red seven. Losing my appetite for feedback, I closed the screen and aimed the remote control at the television even though I didn't need to, even though I could have just blindly hit "OK" from the crevice between the sofa cushions where the blue tooth remote control had fallen when I'd sat down to eat.

Q & P

are
the
initials
of a pedophile
serial
killer
in a Joyce
Carol
Oates
novel.

As far as
pet names
go,
we
picked
a winner,

naming
our-
selves
after
the un-
canny
eponym,

a doll
with arms
wide open,
dilated
eyes,
a kind of de-
ranged
hospitality
marked
with a
question
mark
swirl
at the pinnacle
of the fore-

head.
Mass
produced
plastic
      affect-
       ion.

Pet names
lend them-
  selves to
       lovers,
  automatic re-
flex,
whether
you're there
  or not.

      P
      is for
psycho-
sis,
   love
sui-
 cide
 pact,
   life
part-
 ner,
      peas
 in
 a
  pod,
phallic
 im-
pro-
 priety,
 pleasure
  domes
  and
   pleas-
  ure
 quart-
  ers,

and
pill-
ows,

prep-
arations for
end
of life
care.

Q
is for
occasio-
nal
dis-
content
for quilts,
pin-
cushion
kiss-
es,
quest
for
fire
crotch,
the beau-
tiful
quim,
membr-
anous
mem-
ory
of
an
or-
if-
ice,
cold
plast-
ic
ex-
plosives,
com-

fort-
   able
queens,
            fear-
   less,
      ever-
   y
night,
         to
   cuddle
   up
      with
a
            sex-
         ual
      pre-
da-
tor
   for
eve-
   r.

Night writing

—late coming
—laid another night another alert
—I ate some other butter under jelly on a corn cracker
—fire acher
—it better get its
—the gift gets better
—lucky chatter
—bear batter
—black boxer shorts shirts
—late reading is not really writing
—a birthday ladder blows out a nephew
—all this all in one night
—give me something to be read in
—faceless pup
—a lint in a linked account
—frosted chain
—fortune's in search of a fridge
—nun for all
—messy bottom for nonchalance
—these seeds are in me
—"water closet"
—we need to talk about looking for
—a writing before bed
—pleas respond
—remote control books
—unanswered and blocked
—cold comfort

In the land of gods & monsters

We listened to Lana channel
all the queen's men, singing
"Alleluia" and slurring all the
esses, obliterating the bees
with bilabial lassitude. I called
it honey, "The Great Lana
                Slowdown," pop
music's impossible sap. We
learned to murder the inner
critics, cut bad drag from the
homemade patterns, blasted
the music and drank gin.
Dancing in the kitchen with
passive ears to hear
the sermons of latter day
saints over dinner. "Sin, but sin
boldly." (Yes because —
a little time for ourselves is all
this was

& So

this cage
            for me
is a song to sing

of our
            daily destination
    toward the television
    set

O night
            sexless night

    here we are we two alone
            coughing in and out of phase

I want
            nothing
    you are
            this night
    enough

Come to bed
                put out
            once and for all
    that cigarette

you hold
    my hand, my voice
        my lungs

                I hear you

I'll bring
    the water and we'll
        fall
    exhaling
            our own tempos
evangelically

We sleep
            talk

confessing in solemn intervals
    that we're happy
  in this
      canon

This bareback is for all of us

Rubbing against the grain of infection
is less painful   flat palms on new felt

All I ever wanted was to preserve you
in this slip and slide   be still

I draw the illusion from you like poison
from a wounded ego

The contact feels important   or if not
important   generous

Everybody circles around the potluck
taking turns at the casserole

I don't know why we're lucky enough
to have this chance   it's the same system
only now it has decided that we can live

Someone spread the word about all this
barebacking in America   Tell them
that we're working together again   at last
the old gay power

A book of possible titles
after Jill Johnston

begins a world.
No more order. I'm tired
of breaking things.

Refrain from refrain.
Please remember to
be all those bad times

breaking things.
Don't be narrow,
refrain from refrain.

Even repeating's queer,
feels unright, sounds
of breaking things.

A book of possible titles
is all you need.
Resuscitate your work.

Be all those bad times.
Being horny and lonely
is all you need.

We forgot who we were
on the highway
of breaking things.

No more order. I'm tired.
A funny found source
begins a world.

Ryan Tracy is a writer, composer, performer, and scholar. His criticism and fiction have appeared in *Arizona Quarterly*, *Derrida Today*, *PANK*, *The American Reader*, *The New York Press*, *The Brooklyn Rail*, *Mouvement* (France), *Performa Magazine*, and *The Gay and Lesbian Review*. His poetry has appeared in *The New Engagement*, *California Quarterly*, *CafeMo*, and *Calliope*.